TRADING FOR BEGINNERS

Forex Trading: The Beginner's Guide

Table of Contents

Introduction 1

Chapter 1: What is Forex Trading? 3

Chapter 2: The Benefits and Risks of Forex Trading 13

Chapter 3: How to Get Started in the Forex Market 23

Chapter 4: Forex Trading Strategies 31

Chapter 5: Creating a Trading Plan 45

Chapter 6: The Mindset of the Forex Trader 53

Chapter 7: Reducing Your Risks in Forex Trading 59

Conclusion 67

INTRODUCTION

Congratulations on downloading this book and thank you for doing so.

The following chapters will discuss everything that you need to know to get started with the forex market. Forex trading allows you to trade in currencies around the world and you get the option of trading any currency pair that you would like. This provides you with a ton of options to really increase your profits and to have some changes and fun along the way.

This guidebook will spend some time talking about how to invest in the forex market. You will learn some of the basics of the forex market, some of the best strategies that will help you be successful, the benefits and the risks of forex trading, and even how to create your own trading plan to see the best results. We will end the guidebook with some tips on how to reduce your risks so that you can earn as much profit as possible in the forex market.

Trading in the forex market can be a great way to increase your portfolio and to earn a profit. When you are ready to get started with fore trading, make sure to check out this guidebook to learn everything you need to know to get started and making a profit today.

There are plenty of books on this subject on the market, thanks again for choosing this one! Every effort was made to ensure it is full of as much useful information as possible. Please enjoy!

CHAPTER 1

WHAT IS FOREX TRADING?

Picking out a good investment option can be a challenge for many people. You want to pick something that will make them a lot of money, but you want to ensure that your risk is as limited as possible so you won't lose money at all. You can choose to work with day trading, you can invest in your retirement plan, you can choose to get into real estate, and you can choose to start your own business. Each of these can bring you a profit, and carry some risk, depending on how well you manage them.

One option that you can choose is to invest in Forex trading. The forex market is a global market where you can purchase and sell any currency throughout the world. You can purchase a currency from Europe, from Japan, from China, or anywhere else that you would like. This market was opened during the 1970s when free exchange rates were established. Since the market opened, businesses and people have participated in the forex market, and they have been able to determine what price one currency will have to counter another currency based on supply and demand.

When it comes to the forex market, you are working with free trade because it is working without any outside control. Anyone who would like to try out forex trading can do so, and they compete with others who are in the market. Plus, investors will be able to choose whether they want to enter into a new transaction or not. There isn't anyone who is forcing them to get into the market, and they can always take a break whenever they would like.

Forex trading has many transactions that are carried out each day, which makes this one of the most liquid monetary markets in the whole world. Several studies show that the volume of money that is traded on this market is almost five trilling USD each day. This is a huge amount of money and means that you can earn a ton of profit if you learn how to work this market the profit way.

One nice thing about working with forex trading is that you can conduct this kind of investment no matter where you are from. As long as you have the internet and a telecommunications network, you can join the forex market whenever works the best for you. Unlike the traditional business hours that come with the stock market, the forex market operates 24 hours a day, five days a week. You won't be able to trade over the weekend, but you can exchange currencies any time you would like from 00:00 GMT on Monday to 22:00 GMT on Friday.

Many traders are worried about joining the forex market because they don't want a few big participants getting into the market and controlling the whole thing. This is not likely to happen simply because of the sheer volume of transactions that occur on the market. Even if there were a few participants who wanted to control the market and alter the prices in this market, they would need to be able to invest billions of dollars to make this happen. Most investors do not have that much money available to invest, and so the forex market maintains its neutrality. In addition, because of the high volume of money that flows in and out of the market each day, the forex market is easily able to bounce back after a big economic event.

Each forex trading transaction will be completed through separate contracts, which are called lots. The typical size of one of these contracts or lots is 100,000 units. This shows that if you acquire one typical sized contract, you will be able to control a base currency that has a total quantity of 100,000 units. Then each of these contracts can be subdivided into pips, which will pertain to the minimum price increment. Standard lots have a pip value of $10, but for those who are just getting started with forex trading, you can sometimes try out a mini-account (which some forex companies offer), and then you may be able to pay $1 or less for this.

As you can see, compared to working in the stock market, the forex trading market requires a lot lower margin, especially when you learn how to use leverage to your advantage. In forex trading, you will not be obligated to purchase the currency, making it easier to trade it later on without coming up with a bunch of money upfront. You can open up a forex position to purchase or sell a particular currency, even if you do not own that currency.

For example, you can open up a forex account with an internet broker by setting up a deposit of $2000. With this minimum deposit, you can trade using the 1:100 leverage. What this means is that you can open a position amounting to $200,000, but you only need to invest $2000. The rest would be a credit. This can be nice for those who would like to get started in forex trading, but who don't have a ton of money to work to begin.

What is forex?

Now that we have taken a look at forex a little bit and seen some of the benefits that come with this investment option, it is time to delve deeper into it. The foreign exchange market, or forex, is basically a place where currencies are traded. Currencies can be important to most people around the world because these currencies are needed to conduct business and even foreign trade. For example, if you live in the United States and you would like to purchase cheese from France, you or the company who will purchase the cheese for you, will need to pay in Euros for this cheese.

For this to happen, the U.S. importer would need to take their USD and exchange it for the equivalent in Euros. This is also what you will see when it comes to traveling. If a French tourist is traveling to Egypt, they would not be able to use Euros to purchase some food or to go on a tour since Euros are not a currency is accepted in that country. For the French tourist to make purchases in Egypt, they would need to exchange their Euros for the Egyptian pound (or whichever currency is accepted locally where they are visiting), using the current exchange rate.

The need for individuals and businesses to exchange currencies is one of the biggest reasons that the forex market is the largest and most liquid financial market in the whole world. It dwarfs other markets, including the stock market, because so many people are constantly exchanging out currencies to use for various reasons.

One aspect that you will find unique about the forex market is that there is not a central marketplace for this exchange. Instead, these currencies are traded using an electronic over the counter system. What this means is that all of the transactions that occur in the forex market will occur via an online network between the traders around the world, rather than in one centralized exchange. This allows the market to be open 24 hours a day during the regular work week and these currencies are traded throughout the world in all the major financial institutions including London, Paris, Hong Kong, Frankfurt, and more.

There are three main ways that individuals, corporations, and institutions can trade forex. These include the futures market, the forwards market, and the spot market. The spot market is one of the largest in forex trading because it is the underlying real asset that the futures and forwards markets will be based on. In the past, it would be the futures market that most people choose because it allowed individual investors more time to trade. For most individuals, the spot market is the best option to go with, while companies that are hedging their risks in forex will work with the futures and forwards markets.

What is the spot market

The spot market is where the currencies will be purchased and sold based on their current price. That price will be determined by the current supply and demand for that currency and may include many factors including sentiment about political situations in the country, economic performance, and current interest rates. In some cases, it could be the perception of how the currency will do in the future based on another currency.

With this option, when a deal is finalized, it is often called a spot deal. This transaction is bilateral which means that one party will deliver an agreed-upon currency amount to the other party and then will receive a specified amount of another currency at the exchange rate value. After these positions are closed, the settlement will be in cash. While this spot market is the one that deals with the transactions that occur here in the present, it can take a few days to reach the settlement.

Forwards and futures market

Unlike the spot market that we just talked about, the forwards and futures markets will not trade with the actual currencies. Instead, they will deal with contracts that will represent a claim to a type of currency, a specific price for each unit, and a future date for settling.

With the forwards market, the contracts will be purchased and sold over the counter between two parties. These two parties will set out the terms of agreement that they both like before continuing.

With the futures markets, futures contracts are purchased and sold based on the standard size and settlement date that is found on the public commodities markets. Futures contracts have some specific details in them, including how many units are being traded, the dates for delivery and settlement, and the minimum price increments, which will not be customizable. The exchange will act like a counterpart to the trader because it provides clearance and settlement.

Both of these contracts are binding, and they will typically be settled for cash once the expiry is reached. However, these contracts can be purchased and sold before they expire. These two markets can also offer the investor some protection against the risks when they are trading in currencies. In most cases, you will find big corporations using these markets to protect themselves against some exchange rate fluctuations, but there are a lot of speculators who will take part in these markets as well.

Working with the forex market can be a great way for you to make an income off other currencies. You will find that there is a huge amount of liquidity that comes with the forex market and if you learn how these currencies work and can learn when one will increase in value compared to another currency, and you will be able to make money in no time.

CHAPTER 2

THE BENEFITS AND RISKS OF FOREX TRADING

Working with forex trading can be an exciting endeavor. It allows you the opportunity to invest your money and, with a little time and effort, you will be able to earn a profit. You do need to be careful though and learn how to read the market. This is an investment and just because you place your money into the market does not automatically mean you will earn a profit in the process. However, those who learn how the market works and who are willing to put in the time and effort to make smart predictions about future markets will find that trading in the forex market can help them make a lot of money.

If you are considering getting started in the forex market, there are a lot of things to consider. Let's take a look at some of the benefits and some of the risks that come with forex trading so you can make a well-informed decision before investing.

The benefits of forex trading

To start, we will look at the benefits of forex trading. There are many of them, and if you are ready to branch out with your trading, or want an exciting place to get started, then this is definitely the place for you. Some of the benefits that you will get from forex trading include:

- 24-hour market: Since the forex market is available worldwide, you will be able to trade at any time, as long as there is a market open someplace throughout the world. Trading will start when the market opens on Sunday evening in Australia, and it will end after it closes in New York on Friday. This gives you plenty of opportunities to invest in the market on a schedule that works the best for you.

- High Liquidity: Liquidity is important when it comes to investing, whether you are working with day trading, the stock market, or some other investment. Liquidity is basically the ability of an asset to be converted back to cash quickly without any price discount. It is your ability to get out of the trade, hopefully for a profit, at any time that you would like. If there aren't a lot of people interested in the market, the liquidity is low because there aren't a lot of buyers and sellers. With the forex market, you can move large amounts of money into and out of the market without a ton of price movement.

- Low transaction costs: With other investments, you have to worry about how much it costs to get into the trade. With Forex, you will find that the cost of your transaction will be built into the price that you pay. This is known as the spread, and it is the difference between the purchase and the sale price.

- Option to use leverage: Brokers with forex will be able to allow their traders to use leverage when trading in this market. What this means is that you can trade more money than what you have in your account. So if you are to trade at a 50:1 leverage you would be able to trade $50 on the market for every $1 in your account. Of course, there is some risk in this if you lose. But it does make it easier for beginners with little capital to get started.

- Profit potential no matter which way the market is going: When you trade on the forex market, you will find that there are no restrictions for directional trading. If you think that a currency pair will increase in value, you get the choice to purchase it or go long. In addition, if you feel that it may decrease in value, you have the choice to sell it or to go short. You can make profits on both these decisions.

- Lots of choices: You can choose which currency pair you would like to work with. If you want to trade USD for Euro, you can do that, or you can pick another currency to work with. You can also switch between a few options. If you get into the market and your currency is not going well, you can switch to another currency that is rising in value based on your beginning currency. This can help to reduce the risks that you are dealing with in this market.

- Anyone can join: Whether you are using our own capital or utilizing leverage, you will find that it is easy to join the forex market. Many people are already joining it because of the potential profit and the limited risk that they can face when they do this the right way.

- No one controls the market: It is nearly impossible for any large entity to come into the forex market and take control. This is because there is just too much money going in and out for anyone to do this. If an entity or group wanted to control the forex market, they would need to have billions of dollars to make this happen. Most people do not want or have this much to invest, so they won't worry about controlling this market.

As you can see, there are a lot of potential benefits that you will be able to get when it comes to trading on the forex market. You do need to do the right research ahead of time and take care to read charts and understand the market. But when it is compared to many other investment options, this is one of the best choices that you can make to put your money to work for you.

The risks of forex trading

While there are a lot of great benefits to trading in forex, there are a few risks that you need to be aware of. This is a type of investment so while you can earn a good profit if you play the market the right way, you have to be aware that there are times when the market will not go your way, or that you make a poor decision, and you will lose money in the process. Let's take a look at some of the risks that come with forex trading and how you can avoid them to see the best results with your investment.

The first risk that you will see with forex trading is the risk with leverages. This is seen as a benefit for some people because they can invest more, and possibly earn more, than what they have readily available inside their accounts. However, when you are investing more money than you have in your account, you are increasing your risks as well. Small fluctuations in price can result in a margin call where the investor will need to pay an additional margin. During market conditions that are more volatile, aggressively using leverage can often result in big losses. These losses will often be a lot more than what you initially invested and can cost you big if you are not careful.

Another risk is interest rates. The interest rate will have a big effect on the exchange rate that a country can offer. If the interest rate rises, the currency will strengthen because there is an influx of investors to that country. This happens because the stronger currency means the investor will earn higher profits. On the other hand, if the interest rate falls, the currency of that country will fall, and many investors will start to withdraw their investments. You are taking a risk when you get started that these interest rates will go up or down.

Transaction risks are another risk that is associated with the time differences between when our contract begins and when it settles. This kind of trading occurs on a 24-hour basis, which means that the exchange rates can change before your trade has had time to settle. In addition, currencies may be traded at different times and prices during the same trading hours. Remember that the larger the time difference is between entering and settling your contract, the bigger the risk of the transaction will be. Any difference in time will allow for this risk to fluctuating, and the costs can often take away your profit.

You can also run into risks with the counterparty that you work with. The counterparty is the company that will provide you with the asset. The counterparty risk that you deal with can be the risk of default from the broker or dealer in a particular transaction. When you work in fore, the forward contracts on currencies will not be guaranteed by a clearinghouse or exchange. With spot trading, this type of risk will come from the solvency of the market maker. When the market conditions are volatile, the counterparty may not be able to, or they may refuse, to adhere to your contracts and you will be the one who loses out.

When you are picking out which currency to invest in, you need to consider the stability and structure of your issuing country. In many of the developing countries that you may want to work with, the exchange rates are fixed to those of a world leader, such as the US dollar. In these circumstances, central banks are required to sustain adequate reserves to maintain a fixed exchange rate. In some cases, the currency crisis will occur because of the frequent balance of payment deficits, and this can devalue the currency. Overall, this will have a big effect on the prices that you can get for the currency.

It is never a good idea to go for a currency that is not going to increase in value and picking one from a developing country that is not doing that well can be a challenge. However, these countries have the biggest room to grow as their value will often start out small compared to the USD, so there is more potential for earning a profit if you go with these. Due to the speculative nature of forex trading, you have to watch the market well so that you can get out quickly enough. If an investor thinks that the value of their currency will decrease, they may want to withdraw their assets, which devalues the currency even more. Staying in the market may mean that your assets will lose their liquidity and you may need to deal with insolvency from your dealer. This is a huge risk because you will be stuck with a currency that is worthless or you will only be able to earn pennies on the dollar when you do exchange it out.

There are many reasons why you would want to trade in the forex market, but it is still important to understand some of the risks that come with this kind of investment. Forex trading is a great way to make some money and put your money to work for you, but there are a number of risks that you need to focus on and try to avoid. This helps you to avoid issues later on and can ensure that you will avoid these risks as much as possible to earn more money in this market.

CHAPTER 3

HOW TO GET STARTED IN THE FOREX MARKET

Now that you know a little bit more about forex trading and what the market is all about, it is time to get your account set up. You will be able to work with your broker and pick out your strategy so that the trade will be successful. Anyone can join the forex market and exchange out currencies, which is part of the reason that this is such a liquid market. When you are ready to get started with investing in this market, make sure to do the following steps to help you get going.

Pick a broker

One of the most important things that you can do when getting into the forex market is to find a good broker.

Keeping up with the currencies in other countries can be difficult for a beginner and a broker will be able to walk you through the process. There are many different types of brokers, and it will often depend on how much help you need to get started and how much you want to pay for the broker.

Some investors will choose a broker to use their platform and get some of the benefits, but they do not need the broker for anything else. Many brokers are willing to provide you with the platform that you need, and you can usually get these services at a discount. If you have invested in the past and you have a good idea of how to work with the forex market, then this may be the best option for you.

However, if you are new to forex investing, or even investing in general, it is best to work with a more full-service broker. This broker will not only be able to provide you with a platform but also with any advice and help that you need. Any time that you have questions or you need some help finishing a trade, the broker can be there to help you out. These brokers will often charge a bit more in fees, but they can help you get a good start when you are new to forex trading.

Set up an account

Once you have found a broker you would like to work with, you need to set up your account with them. Most people choose to go with an account through their broker, even if they are doing most of the work on their own. These accounts often have some extra features available, such as better options for leveraging, chances to try out forex trading ahead of time, and more.

Your broker should be able to help you set up your own account. You will need to provide some personal information and link up a bank account to help you get started and to receive your payments. This information will also be presented to the IRS at the end of the year showing your profits and losses so filling it all out completely.

Once the account is set up, take some time to look around. This will help you to see how the dashboard is set up and you can ask any questions that you have before you get started. The more familiar you are with your account, the easier it will be to join the forex market and see results.

Pick your strategy

No matter which type of investment you choose to go with, you need to make sure that you have a strategy in place. These strategies are important because they help to limit your risk if you use them properly. You also get the benefit of knowing exactly what you need to get done during the trade.

There are a lot of good strategies that you can use, and most of them have a chance of being successful based on how you use them and what kind of market you are working with. These strategies can tell you when to enter the market, when to leave the market, and how to react whether you are earning money or losing money in the process.

We will discuss some of the best strategies to use later in this guidebook, and you can pick the one that you think will work the best for you. You can stick with something that is simple to use or go with a more complicated option. The most important thing to remember is that when you pick a strategy, you need to stick with it the whole trade. Trying to mix and match strategies or switching from one strategy to another during the same trade is a surefire way to lose all your money during that trade.

Do a fundamental analysis

If you have worked in the stock market before, you know that a fundamental analysis is important to help you pick out good stocks to work with. This helps you to figure out how well a company is doing and how they will do in the future, based on who runs the company, the product and more. It can often help you to figure out which companies are undervalued and will possibly see an increase in price in the near future.

With forex trading, you will need to do a fundamental analysis as well. But instead of dealing with one company, you are doing this analysis to value a whole country. This makes the analysis more complex, but it can be used to predict long-term trends. There are some that will only need to do this based on news releases, but there are a lot of different things that you can look at to figure out whether the currency is worth your time with a fundamental analysis.

The good news is that there are many indicators that will help you to figure out the value of your currency. Some of these include:

- Durable goods

- Retail sales

- Consumer price index

- Purchasing managers index

- Non-farm payrolls

Of course, these are not the only fundamental factors that you can watch. You can also look at who is running the country, the goods this country produces, how others feel about this country and more. You basically want to figure out how the country runs and how others feel about the country overall to determine if this is the right currency to invest in for you.

Getting into the forex market is not a complicated thing. Many people choose to go in the market just so they can make purchases or so they can travel to another country and visit for a bit. But if you would like to earn a profit in the forex market, you will need to take a few more steps to get started. But when you pick out a good broker and have the right strategy, you will see results in no time.

CHAPTER 4

FOREX TRADING STRATEGIES

Before you decide to enter the forex market, you need to pick out the strategy that you want to use. Without a good strategy, you are just putting your money in and hoping that it all works out for you. Unfortunately, this often goes the other way, and you will lose out on a lot of money, especially if you used leverage to help you get going. The good news is there are many different strategies that you can choose for forex trading, and they can all be successful if you use them properly.

The most common trading strategies for the forex market can be placed in one of two groups: long-term trading or short-term trading. When you work with long-term trading, the trader will base their analysis on the data and charts they get at the end of the day, and then you will maintain that same position for at least a few weeks, if not longer. The long-term trader is basically going to spend time monitoring the trends in the market.

One big advantage to going with a long-term trade is that you will not need to monitor the market as much and you would not need to do as many trade transactions. This can save you a lot of time or money. Most long-term traders do not need to have elaborate software to help them analyze the trends as well because the market trends are not going to be as important. However, you do need to deal with bigger stops in your trade, and there is the risk of a big equity swing while you are in the market.

You can also choose to work as a short-term trade. With these trades, you will need to base your analysis on intraday information and data and the trade is only going to last for up to two weeks at most. It is often called swing trading, and you can even limit your trading to just one day. The aim here is to earn a bunch of small profits with the price swings that happen throughout the day.

The biggest advantage of working with short-term trading is that you get to take advantage of many different trading opportunities that occur during the day. You may not earn a ton on each trade, but when you make a bit of money each day, you will be less likely to have a losing month. You do need to be aware of the higher transaction fees that you will incur for all of these trades.

Both of these can help you to make money in the forex market. You will get to decide which one will work the best for your needs and how much time you want to spend looking at the market. There are a number of strategies that you can use that fit into the short-term and long-term categories. Let's take a look at some of the best forex trading strategies that you can use to help you make a profit in this market.

Scalping

The main objective of scalping is to earn small profits at frequent intervals from the price movements that happen in the market. In some cases, you can use scalping to enter and then exit a trade within a few minutes or less. You are not going to earn huge profits from each trade, but when you do this many times throughout the day, it can add up to big profits by the end. Depending on how much time you want to spend on scalping, you could do between twenty and over a hundred transactions in one day.

This is a risky type of trading strategy. You have to hope that you can get the currency at a lower price and then sell it within a few minutes for a higher price to make a profit. You also need to make enough to cover all your transaction fees as well. However, the level of risk that you get with scalping can sometimes change based on the market that you use and the time of day that you complete the transactions. You will see the most success with scalping when you do it during trending conditions and the best time to trade is when the market is varying within consolidation patterns.

To see success with scalping, you will need to react and make decisions quickly. This requires a lot of time looking at the market and understanding when trends are about to happen. Since scalping allows you to do a lot of different trades in the market, it is a good idea to take any of the profit opportunities that are presented to you.

Sometimes these will be in small amounts, but that can add up quickly.

Intraday trading

Another option that you can go with is known as intraday trading. With this option, you will enter a position at the beginning of the day and then you will close up all those positions before the end of the day. You will not handle as many transactions with this one as you did with the scalping strategy, which makes it a bit easier for a beginner to handle. For this one to work, you are normally going to analyze a trade and then complete it within a short timeframe. Usually, these timeframes will work with charts that follow half an hour to an hour on the market to help you make your decisions.

Position trading

You can also work with the position trading strategy. With this particular strategy, your objective is to improve your position size in increments while observing the market to ensure that you can keep your risk level at the same level. Some people call this technique "averaging into a position" because you will open a new position in the market. This new position will be a similar size and direction as your other position. You will do this each time that the risks of the previous position can already be covered.

With the help of this position, you are better in control of your exposures and risks because you can keep them level throughout the whole process. This strategy also has the potential to give you high profits while keeping up with a market trend. You would want to use this strategy if you have a longer timeline to invest, but it can be used even if you are working with intraday forex trading. For example, in one day you can add to the position so that you can still collect some profits when you close out at the end of the day without all the risk.

If you are going with position trading, you need to make sure that you are working with smaller lot sizes and that your risk exposure is as low as possible. Most new investors will keep their risk exposure to one or two percent of their total capital investment. What this means is that if your account investment is $1000, you should limit your exposure to $10 to $20 and no more.

The blade runner trade

The blade runner trade is a good strategy to use in the forex market because it will use the price action to find entries. You will use round numbers, support and resistance levels, pivot points, and candlesticks to help you to figure out when to join the market. With all of these market indicators in place, you are more likely to pick out a currency that will provide you with a profit in the fore market. For this one to work, you need to make sure that certain indicators are in place and that you see these indicators in more than one place for the best result. You can also look for important news events concerning your currency to help you make decisions.

The suggested approach to making this one successful is to open up two orders. You want to have a long entry and a short entry to help you make the most profit and to reduce your risks. The steps that you need to do to work on the long entry include:

- 2 buy stop orders that have been placed with entry 2 pips above your confirmatory candle.

- The orders need to expire when the new candle starts.

- The stop loss should then be placed two pips below your signal candle that touched the 20 EMA. This is not set in stone, so if you would like to limit your loss more, then you need to move it up a bit.

- The take profit on your first order should be set at an amount that is equal to the risk of pips. So, if the risk for this trade is 20 pips, the first order's take profit should then be 20 pips as well.

- The take profit on your second order will be equal to double the risk of pips. So, using the example above, your second order should be set at 40 pips.

- Once that order is done, it is time for you to work on the short entry. To do this, use the following steps:

- Place 2 sell stops that are placed with an entry that is to pips below the confirmatory candle.

- The orders need to expire at the start of a new candle.

- Your stop loss is then placed two pips above your signal candle that touched at the 20 EMA. This is not something set in stone, and you can place it after a recent swing point if you like that answer better.

- The take profit will be the other step where the first order will be equal to the risk of pips.

- The take profit on your second order will be equal to double the risk of pips.

Once your price has moved in favor of your trade by an amount that will equal your initial risk, one of the orders will be closed, and then the stop loss will be moved to break even. So, with the example above, once your price is above 20 pips favoring your trade, you would close the first order, and then your new stop loss for the remaining order will be reset to a breakeven.

The stop for the remaining order will be left at this breakeven point until the market closes. Either it will reach the profit target, or it will stop out at the breakeven. If you feel that there is a big news announcement that is about to happen, you may decide to continue trailing the stop beyond your breakeven point.

Bolly Band Bounce Trade

Many beginners like to work with an obvious trend because it is more straightforward to working in a range bound or with a price that is moving sideways. However, there are some strategies that will help you cope with price range movements that are more restricted, and the Bolly Band Bounce trade will be one of these that can help you. These are well named because they will exhibit a kind of elasticity that is similar to what you find in rubber bands. Price will approach an outer band, and then they will come up with a resistance before snapping back to the opposite band.

One way to make this behavior work the best for you is to trade the bounces at the outer bands. If the market is sharply trending, this is not the most effective option. But when the market is staying within a range, this is a good option to help with short-term scalps.

Before going with this strategy, you need to determine what your price for the currency is actually staying in a range. There are some different ways to do this, but one of the easiest is to check if the price is staying on one side or the other of your mid-band. If you see this and you can tell that the price is consistently making lower lows, then your price is trending down. The opposite will occur when working with an uptrend.

The idea of this strategy to use it when the market is quiet and when you are not expecting some fundamental news announcements to happen. Spiky price actions will go against this trade and can make you lose out on money. And of course, make sure that you do not enter into a trade with this strategy based only on the fact that the price is reaching an outer band. You need to also look for a confluence at your outer band and then enter the market and see profits.

The Blade Runner Reversal

This is a variation of the Blade runner strategy that we talked about before, but it will rely on the polarity indicator. This indicator is a combination of the

Bollinger mid-band and the 20 EMA, so it is a good combination of the two strategies that we already talked about. If you are not able to get access to a polarity indicator (talk to your broker to see if they have this available), then you could just use these two factors to help you out.

The pattern that you are looking for in this one is that the price will break out of its channel and then will trend in one direction or another with some strength for a bit. The trend will then stall and reverse, passing back through that polarity indicator before it comes back to retest the indicator going the other direction.

You may wonder what the difference between the Blade Runner and the Blade runner reversal. The Blade Runner waits for a trend to be confirmed and then will trade bounces from the indicator in the same direction of the trend. But with the Blade runner reversal, you will start using this strategy when the trend is complete, and the price starts to reverse to the other side. Both of these strategies will trade in the direction of the trend based on the closing price of the currency.

You may want to consider employing both the Blade runner reversal along with the Blade runner strategy at the same time. This is a good way to cope with prices that do not keep up with a trend for a good period of time. When they work together, you will find that they make an effective EMA scalping strategy.

These are just a few of the strategies that you can try out when working with forex trading. It often depends on how long you would like to remain in the market and how much money you can spend. Remember that some of them will cost a lot more than the others and, while you can work with leveraging, that is a big risk on its own. Make sure to review the different strategies and see which one can provide you with the best chance of success.

CHAPTER 5

CREATING A TRADING PLAN

Picking out a strategy is one of the most important things that you can do when it comes to forex trading. It will ensure that you are entering the market at the right times, spending enough money that you are comfortable and will still make a profit, and will tell you when to leave the market. With the right strategy, you will have everything spelled out for you from the beginning, and there won't be a lot of questions while you are trading.

The next step though is to create a trading plan. Creating one of these trading plans is not able to guarantee that you will make a profit each time you trade in this market, but without it, you are putting your money at risk. With a good trading plan, you can avoid big mistakes when you trade and sometimes these plans can help you to find a new solution if a mistake does happen. A trading plan will provide you with the right knowledge and tools so that you can react to any results in your trade.

If you set up this trading plan the proper way, you will basically set up all the steps that you should go through when completing your trade. This is a good thing because it can create discipline and will help you to control your emotions. There are a number of things that you can add to a good trading plan which will help to take out the guesswork and can really make forex trading easier. Some of the things that you should include in your trading plan are:

- The market you would like to work with. Basically, this is the currencies that you would like to purchase and sell. Make sure to list out the pairs. If you are from America, you may want to trade out USD for Euros.

- Position size: You also need to determine how much volume you would like to purchase and sell to the fore market.

- Risks: Everyone is comfortable with a different amount of risk. Before you enter the market, you need to figure out how much of your capital investment are you comfortable losing before each trade.

- Entry: You also need to decide when you would like to start purchasing into the forex market and when you would like to sell. You can decide which market hours are the best for you and which news releases will help you to make your decisions.

- Stop: Before entering the market, you need to determine when you would like to close out your position when it is losing money. Waiting until you are already in the market and losing money is often disastrous. There are many people who will see that their position is not well and will hold on too long in the hopes of seeing a change. This change rarely happens, and it often leads you to lose more money in the process.

- Exit: When do you plan to leave your position when you are earning a profit? This may seem silly because you would want to make as much profit as possible. But having this part in place ensures you don't let your emotions get in the way and that you don't stay in the market too long.

- Strategy: Take some time to outline the strategy that you would like to use at this time. You can talk about when you will purchase, when you will sell, and even which indicators you will look for when making your decisions. Any time you get confused about a position or how you should react to something, you can go back to this plan and see what your goals were.

- Timeframe: The next thing that you should consider is how much profit you think you will earn from a particular position. Make sure this number is reasonable.

- Breakeven point: When you enter into a new position, consider what the breakeven point is while doing that position. This helps you to keep track of whether you are actually making a profit or losing money in the process.

This may seem like a lot of work to get started with a trade, but it is so important to help you think through all of your trades. The more analysis you give to your trades, the more likely you will be able to make a good profit in the process.

Steps to open your forex position

There are a few things that you need to do to open up your forex position. First, you need to take a look at the position you are interested in and determine what happened the previous day with that position. When you look at the prices, do they look over-extended or congested? Are the current prices of your position near the lows and highs from the prior day? These will all help you to determine which position to enter and whether you need to make some adjustments.

While you are doing this, take some time to read through the economic reports and any news that pertains to your position online. You can check to see which gaps happened over a holiday or the weekend. If you see that some big news is about to happen with the currency that you are interested in, it may affect the way that you trade.

With all of this information, you will be able to determine the price bar of the position that you want to enter so that you can predict the perspective direction of the price trend. Let's take a look at some of these options and how they will affect your decisions with forex trading.

- Long (buying) alternative 1: This is a price trend that will go up with a downswing that is higher than the two prior downswings.

- Long (buying) alternative 2: This is known as a secondary price trend. This is when that price trend is falling down, but it will rise up in a direction that is similar to the primary price trend.

- Long (buying) alternative 3: This is when the secondary price trend is falling down, but it will rise up in a direction that is similar to the slop of the moving average price trend.

- Short (selling) alternative 1: This price trend is going down with an upswing that is higher than the two prior upswings.

- Short (selling) alternative 2: This is when the secondary price trend is rising up, but it then goes down in a direction that is similar to the primary price trend.

- Short (selling) alternative 3: This is a secondary price trend that will rise up, but then it will go down in a direction that is similar to the slope of the moving average price trend.

From here, you will be able to decide on the entry prices that you want to use. There are two options that you can go with. For the buy entry price, you will purchase currencies when the market price is over the high level of the signal bar and then up one tick. For the sell entry price, you will sell your currencies when the price is under the low level of the signal bar and then minus a tick.

And finally, you need to decide on your exit strategy. You need to have this in place before you get started. Waiting until you are already in the market can be horrible because then you are in the game and your emotions will dictate your decisions, rather than sound judgment. The goal of this exit strategy is to always make money to remember that when deciding when it is time to exit.

There are a few ways that you can determine when you should exit the market. The first one is that you will exit the market when your profit hits around 60 percent of the average price range. You can also exit one lot after you have earned a full profit. You will need to trail the stop of the second mini-lot to make this work.

CHAPTER 6

THE MINDSET OF THE FOREX TRADER

At this point, you have learned a lot about trading on the forex market. You know that there are many currency combinations that you can choose from based on how they are doing and the ones that interest you the most. You have learned some of the best strategies to work with based on the type of market you want to work with and what fits your investing style. We have even looked at some of the steps that you need to take to create your own trading plan to help you keep on track.

Before you decide to start trading in the forex market, it is important to understand the mindset of a forex trader. Not everyone will be able to do well in this market. Sure, anyone can join, and if you plan to go visit a new country, it is likely that you will get into the market at some time to exchange out your currency for the currency of the country you are visiting. But this market moves and often changes and to make money in it, you need to be able to think quickly, keep up on research, and so much more.

So, what sets a forex trader apart from all the rest? What makes them know how to react to different market conditions? How are they able to read the market and make money while others may lose out on everything in just a few trades?

The first thing that you need to realize when you get into the forex market is that you are not always going to earn a profit. Not all trades will end up profitable for you. It doesn't matter if you are a beginner to forex trading or you have been in the market for a long time; everyone will deal with losses at times. If this idea makes you break out into a sweat and you are not able to afford to lose any of your capital, then it is time to consider a different investment option. The forex market can move up and down quickly and trust in a particular country can change from one day to the next. Those who are not able to keep their heads level are more likely to run into issues, and bigger losses, with their investment.

Having a level head is really important as a forex trader. As you learn the market, it will become easier for you to make smart investment choices. But there are times when the market will go against what you had anticipated. If you let this get to you, you are more likely to stay in the market too long and increase your losses. But if you can keep your wits about you and think things through, you can get out of the market and make other decisions that will help you limit your losses.

You also need to be good at keeping track of all your records as a forex trader. If you are not good at taking notes or you just want to jump from one trade to another, this may not be the best investment for you to choose from. Each time you finish up with a trade, you need to write down information. The more details, the better for this. Consider adding in information such as the entry and exit prices, the time and date of your trade, the stops that you followed, the targeted stops that you set out, and how the trade went.

This really only needs to take a few minutes to accomplish, but it can make a big difference. First, it makes you concentrate on what you are doing during the trade. When you think out the trade, it will make it easier to consider whether you are making good decisions. You can also use this information later on when considering a new trade. Nothing is better than your own experience and writing down what you did in various trades will make it much easier to remember things later on. Another thing that you may want to consider writing down is your emotional status during the trade or some of the reasons that you were entering the trade to start with. All this information can help you to determine if you are making smart trades if there are some weak spots you need to change and more.

You also need to be ready to do a lot of research. You do not live in two countries at once, so it is hard to know how things are changing in the countries you are investing in. You have to research to keep up with what is going on in the world around you so you can determine if it is the right time to enter into a forex trade or not.

Without the proper research, you will have some issues with making good predictions for the trades. You may miss out on important news that could either raise or lower the price of your currency and will greatly affect the trades that you decide to do. For those who like to skip over the research or who just think they can wing this investment, it is best to go with a different option.

You need to be a self-starter as well. There won't be anyone around who will make you do the work. This is an investment, and there is no boss behind you making sure that you invest each day or that you follow the other stops that you need to see success. You can choose to work one day and then take a few days off if things aren't going well. And many people like this freedom. But unless you are motivated to keep going with this investment, you will never make money because no one is there to force you to work.

And finally, you need to have the ability to know when it is time to stop. There will be times when the market does not go well, and it is up to you to take a break after a big loss. It is not just important to leave the market when you start to lose money. But if you feel shaken from a bad trade that emptied your account, you must learn how to walk away and take a break. Entering back into the market too quickly will result in you making big mistakes in your trading. Many investors start working as revenge trading in the hopes to make their money back quickly.

The problem with revenge trading is that once you start trading this strategy, you have let your emotions get in the way. You make decisions to earn your money back, rather than making decisions to help you earn money. Your decisions are not well-thought out, and you end up losing more and more money. Walking away and taking a break after a tough loss can be the best way to regain your thoughts before starting over again.

Working in forex trading can be a great experience. It helps you to invest in the currencies of other countries and earn a money as the values change up and down. Before you get started with forex trading, make sure that you are really going to have the right mindset to make this one work for you.

CHAPTER 7

REDUCING YOUR RISKS IN FOREX TRADING

When it comes to any investment, you will want to reduce your risks as much as possible. No one wants to go into an investment and worry about losing money. They want to go into that investment and know that they will make some money in the process. Forex trading is considered a risky investment, but the number of profits that you can make is even higher. The good news is that there are some steps you can take that will decrease your risk and will make it easier to earn the profits that you deserve.

The first thing that you can do to help manage your risks with forex trading is to never trade any money that you aren't able to afford to lose. There will be times when you will lose money. Even the most experienced traders will lose money on occasion when the market doesn't behave as they predicted. As a beginner, your risk of losing money is even higher. It is easy to fall into the idea of "this won't happen to me" when it comes to losing on your trade, but investing too much can really affect how well you can trade.

What are you going to do if you trade on money that you really can't afford to lose? It is possible, no matter how much you may wish it otherwise, that you will lose all that money. Even the threat of losing that money can affect your trading decisions. Once you risk all that money and start to feel the threat of losing the money, your decision-making skills will start to become compromised, and big mistakes will begin to happen.

The next thing that you should concentrate on is that you want to work with small trades in the beginning. It may be tempting to go for some of the bigger trades and to use leverage to your advantage, but this is setting things up for failure. It is best to always make the trade sizes that you are doing appropriate for your account balance.

This can be hard to stick with when working in forex trading. In the United States, you can make trades at 50:1, but unless you have a big backup fund to help you out, it is not smart to go that big. It is always best to trade what you can do safely without compromising your situation too much. While the 50:1 means that you could open up with $100,000 in trades while only having $2000 in your account, it is not a smart idea to do this. You are risking too much money, and your decisions will be motivated by fear of losing all that money rather than on sound financial advice.

You should also consider using stop losses correctly. A stop loss is an order that will stop you from losing more money than necessary for your account. While you should work on making good decisions based on your research and looking at charts, there will be some trades that won't go the way that you would like. Using these stop losses will help you learn when to cut your losses.

Without a good stop loss in place, it is hard to know when to leave the market. You will get caught up in the trade that you are completing and feel bad that you are losing money in the process. You may want to stay in the market, hoping to get your money back if you stay in long enough. But this doesn't always work the best for you; often the market will continue going down, and you end up losing more money than you are comfortable with.

The stop loss prevents this from happening. You will set a point that you are comfortable with before you even enter the trade. When the market reaches this point, you will leave the market regardless of what it may do in the future. The trick here is to set the stop at a spot that you know the trade is likely to reach if you end up being completely wrong with your trade. This way, you can get out of the market without losing all of your money.

You can think of the stop loss as your emergency exit. You should always work to enter the trades that will make you a profit, but they can come into play when your trade is not going well. This allows you to limit your losses and get out of the market before you lose too much. No one wants to think about losing money with a trade that they enter, but it is much better to know exactly how much you will lose if the trade goes poorly, rather than letting the losses be limitless.

As you can see, most of the steps that you can take to limit your losses will concern keeping the emotions out of your trades. Emotions are the worst thing that you can bring along to one of your trades. As soon as those emotions get into the trade, you will start losing money. This is because you will stop paying attention to your trades and will start making irrational decisions along the way.

For example, if you start losing money, you will feel worried and maybe even anger. You don't want to lose money; you entered the market with the intention of making money. And if the market is really going against your trade, especially if you didn't put down a stop loss, you will start to panic. All of the decisions that you make after this point will be to try and regain your lost profits. This never goes well because the worry and fear will cloud your judgment.

When you make smart decisions and put things in place like the stop loss and never investing more than you can lose, you can keep the emotions out of the game. You can make an informed decision, and you can outline all the steps that you will take in the trade. You will know when to enter the market when to leave the market, and all the other steps in between. The more decisions you can make ahead of time, the safer your investment will be for you.

Trading with only money than you can lose if things go poorly, controlling your risks with a good stop loss, and trading with a lot size that is reasonable will all help you to avoid the biggest risks that come with trading in forex. Of course, there are still times that you will lose money on your trade. But these three things will help you to limit your losses and can even help you make better decisions that can prevent these losses in some cases. As a beginner, it is tempting to take a wild approach to your trading because you are excited to get into the market. And there are trades where this will work. Doing this over the long-term though is just setting yourself up for failure, and it won't be long before your accounts become empty.

As a beginner, it is always best to learn how to keep your risks low. You may not end up with as much profit with each of the trades that you do, but it helps to limit your losses. If you can do this over the long-term, you will actually end up with more money in your pocket than going with riskier options. Forex trading is risky enough. Use the tips in this chapter to take away some of the risks and help you to make as much money as possible.

CONCLUSION

Thank you for making it through to the end of this book, let's hope it was informative and able to provide you with all of the tools you need to achieve your goals whatever they may be.

The next step is to enter the forex market. This market may not be the best option for everyone who is looking for something to invest in, but it is a great way for smart investors to find a challenge and make money all at the same time.

Inside, we have learned some of the basics of forex trading as well as some of the benefits. We also talked about the some of the risks that come with this investment. We looked at some of the ways to enter the market, the best strategies to help us see success, and even how we can reduce your risk.

Investing in the forex market can be a challenge, but it can also bring you a great return on investment.

Finally, if you found this book useful in any way, a review on Amazon is always appreciated!

If you want you can subscribe to our newsletter: http://bit.ly/2EZWzlJ